# SONNETS FROM THE PORTUGUESE

# SONNETS FROM THE PORTUGUESE

## And Other Treasured Poems of
### ELIZABETH BARRETT BROWNING

Selected by Nancy Holmes

HALLMARK EDITIONS

## ELIZABETH BARRETT BROWNING

Elizabeth Barrett was born in 1806 in England. She published her first verse at 14. As a spirited 15-year-old who loved the outdoors she injured her spine while horseback riding. Her health after the accident became progressively worse, and at the same time in her life she lost her mother to a long illness, her beloved brother Bro in a sailing accident, and another brother to a tropical fever.

Even though an invalid, she remained curious about the world and responsive to its changes. She read and wrote steadily. By the early 1840's she was an established poet and a prolific correspondent.

Enfeebled by sickness and wholly dependent on her stern father for comfort, Elizabeth Barrett lived confined to her bedroom. It was there, in 1845, that Robert Browning introduced himself. The British poet courted the invalid for more than a year, overcoming both her father's disapproval and Elizabeth's continuing hesitations. They were secretly married in 1846.

The *Sonnets* Elizabeth had composed during their courtship she gave to her husband in 1849. He recognized immediately not only the extent to which they represented Elizabeth's personal triumph over shyness, but also their universal richness and scope. Today as then, critics and readers alike recognize the *Sonnets from the Portuguese* as Mrs. Browning's greatest contribution to literature, and an intimate and moving expression of the growth of love.

SONNETS FROM THE PORTUGUESE

I thought once how Theocritus had sung
Of the sweet years, the dear and wished for years,
Who each one in a gracious hand appears
To bear a gift for mortals, old or young:
And, as I mused it in his antique tongue,
I saw, in gradual vision through my tears,
The sweet, sad years, the melancholy years,
Those of my own life, who by turns had flung
A shadow across me. Straightway I was 'ware,
So weeping, how a mystic Shape did move
Behind me, and drew me backward by the hair;
And a voice said in mastery while I strove, . .
'Guess now who holds thee?'

                  —'Death!' I said.   But, there,
The silver answer rang . . 'Not Death, but Love.'

## VI

Go from me. Yet I feel that I shall stand
Henceforward in thy shadow. Nevermore
Alone upon the threshold of my door
Of individual life, I shall command
The uses of my soul, nor lift my hand
Serenely in the sunshine as before,
Without the sense of that which I forbore, . .
Thy touch upon the palm. The widest land
Doom takes to part us, leaves thy heart in mine
With pulses that beat double. What I do
And what I dream include thee, as the wine
Must taste of its own grapes. And when I sue
God for myself, He hears that name of thine,
And sees within my eyes, the tears of two.

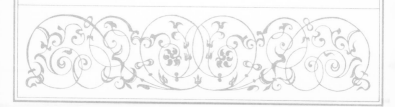

## VII

The face of all the world is changed, I think,
Since first I heard the footsteps of thy soul
Move still, oh, still, beside me; as they stole
Betwixt me and the dreadful outer brink
Of obvious death, where I who thought to sink
Was caught up into love and taught the whole
Of life in a new rhythm. The cup of dole
God gave for baptism, I am fain to drink,
And praise its sweetness, sweet, with thee anear.
The names of country, heaven, are changed away
For where thou art or shalt be, there or here;
And this . . this lute and song . . loved yesterday,
(The singing angels know) are only dear,
Because thy name moves right in what they say.

Yet, love, mere love, is beautiful indeed
And worthy of acceptation. Fire is bright,
Let temple burn, or flax! An equal light
Leaps in the flame from cedar-plank or weed.
And love is fire: and when I say at need
*I love thee*..mark!..*I love thee!*..in thy sight
I stand transfigured, glorified aright,
With conscience of the new rays that proceed
Out of my face toward thine. There's nothing low
In love, when love the lowest: meanest creatures
Who love God, God accepts while loving so.
And what I *feel,* across the inferior features
Of what I *am,* doth flash itself, and show
How that great work of Love enhances Nature's.

Indeed this very love which is my boast,
And which, when rising up from breast to brow,
Doth crown me with a ruby large enow
To draw men's eyes and prove the inner cost, . .
This love even, all my worth, to the uttermost,
I should not love withal, unless that thou
Hadst set me an example, shown me how,
When first thine earnest eyes

                      with mine were crossed,
And love called love. And thus, I cannot speak
Of love even, as a good thing of my own.
Thy soul hath snatched up mine all faint and weak,
And placed it by thee on a golden throne,—
And that I love, (O soul, we must be meek!)
Is by thee only, whom I love alone.

## XIV

If thou must love me, let it be for nought
Except for love's sake only. Do not say
'I love her for her smile . . her look . . her way
Of speaking gently, . . for a trick of thought
That falls in well with mine, and certes brought
A sense of pleasant ease on such a day'—
For these things in themselves, Beloved, may
Be changed, or change for thee,
                                                    — and love so wrought,
May be unwrought so. Neither love me for
Thine own dear pity's wiping my cheeks dry,
A creature might forget to weep, who bore
Thy comfort long, and lose thy love thereby.
But love me for love's sake, that evermore
Thou may'st love on through love's eternity.

## XV

Accuse me not, beseech thee, that I wear
Too calm and sad a face in front of thine;
For we two look two ways, and cannot shine
With the same sunlight on our brow and hair.
On me thou lookest, with no doubting care,
As on a bee shut in a crystalline, —
For sorrow hath shut me safe in love's divine.
And to spread wing and fly in the outer air
Were most impossible failure, if I strove
To fail so. But I look on thee . . on thee . .
Beholding, besides love, the end of love,
Hearing oblivion beyond memory . .
As one who sits and gazes from above,
Over the rivers to the bitter sea.

And yet, because thou overcomest so,
Because thou art more noble and like a king,
Thou canst prevail against my fears and fling
Thy purple round me, till my heart shall grow
Too close against thine heart, henceforth to know
How it shook when alone. Why, conquering
May prove as lordly and complete a thing
In lifting upward as in crushing low:
And as a vanquished soldier yields his sword
To one who lifts him from the bloody earth, —
Even so, Beloved, I at last record,
Here ends my strife. If *thou* invite me forth,
I rise above abasement at the word.
Make thy love larger to enlarge my worth.

Beloved, my Beloved, when I think
That thou wast in the world a year ago,
What time I sat alone here in the snow
And saw no footprint, heard the silence sink
No moment at thy voice, . . but link by link
Went counting all my chains as if that so
They never could fall off at any blow
Struck by thy possible hand. . . . why, thus I drink
Of life's great cup of wonder. Wonderful,
Never to feel thee thrill the day or night
With personal act or speech, — nor ever cull
Some prescience of thee with the blossoms white
Thou sawest growing! Atheists are as dull,
Who cannot guess God's presence out of sight.

## XXI

Say over again and yet once over again
That thou dost love me. Though the word repeated
Should seem 'a cuckoo-song,' as thou dost treat it,
Remember never to the hill or plain,
Valley and wood, without her cuckoo-strain,
Comes the fresh Spring in all her green completed!
Beloved, I, amid the darkness greeted
By a doubtful spirit-voice, in that doubt's pain
Cry. . speak once more. . thou lovest! Who can fear
Too many stars, though each in heaven shall roll —
Too many flowers, though each shall crown the year?
Say thou dost love me, love me, love me — toll
The silver iterance! — only minding, Dear,
To love me also in silence, with thy soul.

## XXII

When our two souls stand up erect and strong,
Face to face, silent, drawing nigh and nigher,
Until the lengthening wings break into fire
At either curved point, — what bitter wrong
Can the earth do to us, that we should not long
Be here contented? Think. In mounting higher,
The angels would press on us, and aspire
To drop some golden orb of perfect song
Into our deep, dear silence. Let us stay
Rather on earth, Beloved, — where the unfit
Contrarious moods of men recoil away
And isolate pure spirits, and permit
A place to stand and love in for a day,
With darkness and the death-hour rounding it.

## XXIV

Let the world's sharpness like a clasping knife
Shut in upon itself and do no harm
In this close hand of Love, now soft and warm;
And let us hear no sound of human strife
After the click of the shutting. Life to life —
I lean upon thee, Dear, without alarm
And feel as safe as guarded by a charm,
Against the stab of worldlings who if rife
Are weak to injure. Very whitely still
The lilies of our lives may reassure
Their blossoms from their roots! accessible
Alone to heavenly dews that drop not fewer;
Growing straight, out of man's reach, on the hill.
God only, who made us rich, can make us poor.

## XXV

A heavy heart, Beloved, have I borne
From year to year until I saw thy face,
And sorrow after sorrow took the place
Of all those natural joys as lightly worn
As the stringed pearls. .each lifted in its turn
By a beating heart at dance-time. Hopes apace
Were changed to long despairs,
                              . .till God's own grace
Could scarcely lift above the world forlorn
My heavy heart. Then *thou* didst bid me bring
And let it drop adown thy calmly great
Deep being! Fast it sinketh, as a thing
Which its own nature doth precipitate,
While thine doth close above it mediating
Betwixt the stars and the unaccomplished fate.

## XXVI

I lived with visions for my company
Instead of men and women, years ago,
And found them gentle mates, nor thought to know
A sweeter music than they played to me.
But soon their trailing purple was not free
Of this world's dust, — their lutes did silent grow,
And I myself grew faint and blind below
Their vanishing eyes. Then THOU
                       didst come . . to *be,*
Beloved, what they *seemed.* Their shining fronts,
Their songs, their splendours . . (better, yet the same,
As river-water hallowed into fonts . .)
Met in thee, and from out thee overcame
My soul with satisfaction of all wants —
Because God's gifts put man's best dreams to shame.

## XXVII

My own Beloved, who hast lifted me
From this drear flat of earth where I was thrown,
And in betwixt the languid ringlets, blown
A life breath, till the forehead hopefully
Shines out again, as all the angels see,
Before thy saving kiss! My own, my own,
Who camest to me when the world was gone,
And I who looked for only God, found *thee!*
I find thee: I am safe, and strong, and glad.
As one who stands in dewless asphodel
Looks backward on the tedious time he had
In the upper life. . so I, with bosom-swell,
Make witness here between the good and bad,
That Love, as strong as Death, retrieves as well.

## XXIX

I think of thee! — my thoughts do twine and bud
About thee, as wild vines about a tree,
Put out broad leaves, and soon there's nought to see
Except the straggling green which hides the wood.
Yet, O my palm-tree, be it understood
I will not have my thoughts instead of thee
Who art dearer, better! Rather instantly
Renew thy presence! As a strong tree should,
Rustle thy boughs and set thy trunk all bare,
And let these bands of greenery which insphere thee
Drop heavily down,.. burst, shattered, everywhere!
Because, in this deep joy to see and hear thee
And breathe within thy shadow a new air,
I do not think of thee — I am too near thee.

## XXXI

Thou comest! all is said without a word.
I sit beneath thy looks, as children do
In the noon-sun, with souls that tremble through
Their happy eyelids from an unaverred
Yet prodigal inward joy. Behold, I erred
In that last doubt! and yet I cannot rue
The sin most, but the occasion...that we two
Should for a moment stand unministered
By a mutual presence. Ah, keep near and close,
Thou dovelike help! and, when my fears would rise,
With thy broad heart serenely interpose!
Brood down with thy divine sufficiencies
These thoughts which tremble when bereft of those,
Like callow birds left desert to the skies.

## XXXII

The first time that the sun rose on thine oath
To love me, I looked forward to the moon
To slacken all those bonds which seemed too soon
And quickly tied to make a lasting troth.
Quick-loving hearts, I thought, may quickly loathe;
And, looking on myself, I seemed not one
For such man's love! — more like an out of tune
Worn viol, a good singer would be wroth
To spoil his song with, and which, snatched in haste,
Is laid down at the first ill-sounding note.
I did not wrong myself so, but I placed
A wrong on *thee*. For perfect strains may float
'Neath master-hands, from instruments defaced, —
And great souls, at one stroke, may do and doat.

## XXXIII

Yes, call me by my pet-name! let me hear
The name I used to run at, when a child,
From innocent play, and leave the cowslips piled,
To glance up in some face that proved me dear
With the look of its eyes. I miss the clear
Fond voices, which, being drawn and reconciled
Into the music of Heaven's undefiled,
Call me no longer. Silence on the bier,
While *I* call God — call God! — So let thy mouth
Be heir to those who are now exanimate:
Gather the north flowers to complete the south,
And catch the early love up in the late!
Yes, call me by that name, — and I, in truth,
With the same heart, will answer, and not wait.

If I leave all for thee, wilt thou exchange
And *be* all to me? Shall I never miss
Home-talk and blessing, and the common kiss
That comes to each in turn, nor count it strange,
When I look up, to drop on a new range
Of walls and floors .. another home than this?
Nay, wilt thou fill that place by me which is
Filled by dead eyes too tender to know change?
That's hardest! If to conquer love, has tried,
To conquer grief tries more . . . as all things prove
For grief indeed is love and grief beside.
Alas, I have grieved so I am hard to love —
Yet love me — wilt thou? Open thine heart wide,
And fold within, the wet wings of thy dove.

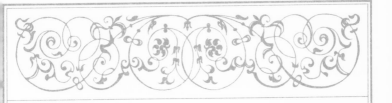

## XXXVIII

First time he kissed me, he but only kissed
The fingers of this hand wherewith I write,
And ever since it grew more clean and white,..
Slow to world-greetings..quick with its 'Oh, list,'
When the angels speak. A ring of amethyst
I could not wear here plainer to my sight,
Than that first kiss. The second passed in height
The first, and sought the forehead, and half missed,
Half falling on the hair. O beyond meed!
That was the chrism of love,

                  which love's own crown,
With sanctifying sweetness, did precede.
The third upon my lips was folded down
In perfect, purple state! since when, indeed,
I have been proud and said, 'My Love, my own.'

## XXXIX

Because thou hast the power and own'st the grace
To look through and behind this mask of me,
(Against which years have beat thus blanchingly
With their rains!) and behold my soul's true face,
The dim and weary witness of life's race: —
Because thou hast the faith and love to see,
Through that same soul's distracting lethargy,
The patient angel waiting for his place
In the new Heavens: because nor sin nor woe,
Nor God's infliction, nor death's neighbourhood,
Nor all which others viewing, turn to go,..
Nor all which makes me tired of all, self-viewed,..
Nothing repels thee,..Dearest, teach me so
To pour out gratitude, as thou dost, good!

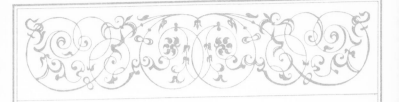

## XLI

I thank all who have loved me in their hearts,
With thanks and love from mine.
                              Deep thanks to all
Who paused a little near the prison-wall,
To hear my music in its louder parts,
Ere they went onward, each one to the mart's
Or temple's occupation, beyond call.
But thou, who in my voice's sink and fall,
When the sob took it, thy divinest Art's
Own instrument didst drop down at thy foot,
To hearken what I said between my tears, . .
Instruct me how to thank thee! — Oh, to shoot
My soul's full meaning into future years,
That *they* should lend it utterance, and salute
Love that endures! with Life that disappears!

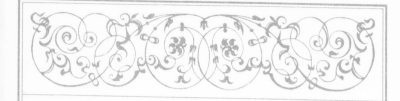

## XLII

Beloved, thou hast brought me many flowers
Plucked in the garden, all the summer through
And winter, and it seemed as if they grew
In this close room, nor missed the sun and showers.
So, in the like name of that love of ours,
Take back these thoughts which here unfolded too,
And which on warm and cold days I withdrew
From my heart's ground. Indeed,

those beds and bowers
Be overgrown with bitter weeds and rue,
And wait thy weeding: yet here's eglantine,
Here's ivy! — take them, as I used to do
Thy flowers, and keep them

where they shall not pine;
Instruct thine eyes to keep their colours true,
And tell thy soul, their roots are left in mine.

## XLIII

How do I love thee? Let me count the ways.
I love thee to the depth and breadth and height
My soul can reach, when feeling out of sight
For the ends of Being and Ideal Grace.
I love thee to the level of every day's
Most quiet need, by sun and candlelight.
I love thee freely, as men strive for Right;
I love thee purely, as they turn from Praise;
I love thee with the passion put to use
In my old griefs, and with my childhood's faith;
I love thee with a love I seemed to lose
With my lost saints, — I love thee with the breath,
Smiles, tears, of all my life! — and, if God choose,
I shall but love thee better after death.

## XLIV

*My future will not copy fair my past.*
I wrote that once; and, thinking at my side
My ministering life-angel justified
The word by his appealing look upcast
To the white throne of God, I turned at last,
And there, instead, saw *thee;* not unallied
To angels in thy soul! Then I, long tried
By natural ills, received the comfort fast,
While budding at thy sight, my pilgrim's staff
Gave out green leaves with
                morning dews impearled.
— I seek no copy now of life's first half!
Leave here the pages with long musing curled,
And write me new my future's epigraph,
New angel mine, unhoped for in the world!

OTHER POEMS

## LOVE

We cannot live, except thus mutually
We alternate, aware or unaware,
The reflex act of life: and when we bear
Our virtue outward most impulsively,
Most full of invocation, and to be
Most instantly compellant, certes, there
We live most life, whoever breathes most air
And counts his dying years by sun and sea.
But when a soul, by choice and conscience, doth
Throw out her full force on another soul,
The conscience and the concentration both
Make mere life, Love. For Life in perfect whole
And aim consummated, is Love in sooth,
As nature's magnet-heat rounds pole with pole.

## WORK AND CONTEMPLATION

The woman singeth at her spinning-wheel
A pleasant chant, ballad or barcarolle;
She thinketh of her song, upon the whole,
Far more than of her flax; and yet the reel
Is full, and artfully her fingers feel
With quick adjustment, provident control,
The lines, too subtly twisted to unroll,
Out to a perfect thread. I hence appeal
To the dear Christian church — that we may do
Our Father's business in these temples murk,
Thus, swift and steadfast; thus, intent and strong;
While, thus, apart from toil, our souls pursue
Some high, calm, spheric tune, and prove our work
The better for the sweetness of our song.

## PATIENCE TAUGHT BY NATURE

'O dreary life!' we cry, 'O dreary life!'
And still the generations of the birds
Sing through our sighing, and the flocks and herds
Serenely live while we are keeping strife
With Heaven's true purpose in us, as a knife
Against which we may struggle. Ocean girds
Unslackened the dry land: savannah-swards
Unweary sweep: hills watch, unworn; and rife
Meek leaves drop yearly from the forest-trees,
To show above the unwasted stars that pass
In their old glory. O thou God of old!
Grant me some smaller grace than comes to *these;* —
But so much patience, as a blade of grass
Grows by contented through the heat and cold.

## THE POET

The poet hath the child's sight in his breast,
And sees all *new*. What oftenest he has viewed,
He views with the first glory. Fair and good
Pall never on him, at the fairest, best,
But stand before him holy and undressed
In week-day false conventions, such as would
Drag other men down from the altitude
Of primal types, too early dispossessed.
Why, God would tire of all his heavens as soon
As thou, O godlike, childlike poet, didst,
Of daily and nightly sights of sun and moon!
And therefore hath He set thee in the midst,
Where men may hear thy wonder's ceaseless tune,
And praise His world for ever, as thou bidst.

## PAIN IN PLEASURE

A thought lay like a flower upon mine heart,
And drew around it other thoughts like bees
For multitude and thirst of sweetnesses;
Whereat rejoicing, I desired the art
Of the Greek whistler, who to wharf and mart
Could lure those insect swarms from orange-trees,
That I might hive with me such thoughts, and please
My soul so, always. Foolish counterpart
Of a weak man's vain wishes! While I spoke,
The thought I called a flower, grew nettle-rough —
The thoughts, called bees, stung me to festering.
Oh, entertain (cried Reason, as she woke,)
Your best and gladdest thoughts but long enough
And they will all prove sad enough to sting.

## TWO SKETCHES

### I

The shadow of her face upon the wall
May take your memory to the perfect Greek;
But when you front her, you would call the cheek
Too full, sir, for your models, if withal
That bloom it wears could leave you critical,
And that smile reaching toward the rosy streak:
For one who smiles so, has no need to speak
To lead your thoughts along, as steed to stall!
A smile that turns the sunny side o' the heart
On all the world, as if herself did win
By what she lavished on an open mart: —
Let no man call the liberal sweetness, sin, —
While friends may whisper, as they stand apart,
"Methinks there's still some warmer place within."

## II

Her azure eyes, dark lashes hold in fee:
Her fair superfluous ringlets, without check,
Drop after one another down her neck;
As many to each cheek as you might see
Green leaves to a wild rose. This sign outwardly,
And a like woman-covering seems to deck
Her inner nature. For she will not fleck
World's sunshine with a finger. Sympathy
Must call her in Love's name! and then, I know,
She rises up, and brightens as she should,
And lights her smile for comfort, and is slow
In nothing of high-hearted fortitude.
To smell this flower, come near it: such can grow
In that sole garden where Christ's brow
                              dropped blood.

## ADEQUACY

Now by the verdure on thy thousand hills,
Beloved England, — doth the earth appear
Quite good enough for men to overbear
The will of God in, with rebellious wills!
We cannot say the morning-sun fulfills
Ingloriously its course; nor that the clear
Strong stars without significance insphere
Our habitation. We, meantime, our ills
Heap up against this good; and lift a cry
Against this work-day world, this ill-spread feast,
As if ourselves were better certainly
Than what we come to. Maker and High Priest,
I ask thee not my joys to multiply, —
Only to make me worthier of the least.

## LESSONS FROM THE GORSE

'To win the secret of a weed's plain heart.'
*Lowell*

Mountain gorses, ever golden!
Cankered not the whole year long!
Do you teach us to be strong,
Howsoever pricked and holden
Like your thorny blooms, and so
Trodden on by rain and snow
Up the hill-side of this life, as bleak as
              where ye grow?

Mountain blossoms, shining blossoms!
Do ye teach us to be glad
When no summer can be had,
Blooming in our inward bosoms?
*Ye,* whom God preserveth still,
Set as lights upon a hill
Tokens to the wintry earth that Beauty
              liveth still!

Mountain gorses, do ye teach us
From that academic chair
Canopied with azure air,
That the wisest word Man reaches
Is the humblest he can speak?
*Ye,* who live on mountain peak,
Yet live low along the ground, beside
      the grasses meek!

Mountain gorses! since Linnaeus
Knelt beside you on the sod,
For your beauty thanking God, —
For your teaching, ye should see us
Bowing in prostration new.
Whence arisen, — if one or two
Drops be on our cheeks — O world! they are
      not tears, but dew.

## HEAVEN AND EARTH

'And there was silence in heaven for the space of half-an-hour.'
*Revelation*

God, who, with thunders and great voices kept
Beneath thy throne, and stars most silver-paced
Along the inferior gyres, and open-faced
Melodious angels round; — canst intercept
Music with music; — yet, at will, hast swept
All back, all back, (said he in Patmos placed,)
To fill the heavens with silence of the waste,
Which lasted half-an-hour! — Lo, I who have wept
All day and night, beseech Thee by my tears,
And by that dread response of curse and groan
Men alternate across these hemispheres,
Vouchsafe us such a half-hour's hush alone,
In compensation for our stormy years!
As heaven has paused from song,

                     let earth, from moan.

## STANZAS

I may sing; but minstrel's singing
Ever ceaseth with his playing.
I may smile; but time is bringing
Thoughts for smiles to wear away in.
I may view thee, mutely loving;
But *shall* view thee so in dying!
I may sigh; but life's removing,
And with breathing endeth sighing!

Be it so!


When no song of mine comes near thee,
Will its memory fail to soften?
When no smile of mine can cheer thee,
Will thy smile be used as often?
When my looks the darkness boundeth,
Will thine own be lighted after?
When my sigh no longer soundeth,
Wilt thou list another's laughter?

Be it so!

You see this dog. It was but yesterday
I mused forgetful of his presence here,
Till thought on thought drew
                      downward tear on tear;
When from the pillow, where wet-cheeked I lay,
A head as hairy as Faunus, thrust its way
Right sudden against my face, — two golden-clear
Great eyes astonished mine, — a drooping ear
Did flap me on either cheek to dry the spray!
I started first, as some Arcadian,
Amazed by goatly god in twilight grove:
But as my bearded vision closelier ran
My tears off, I knew Flush, and rose above
Surprise and sadness; thanking the true Pan,
Who, by low creatures, leads to heights of love.

## FINITE AND INFINITE

The wind sounds only in opposing straights,
The sea, beside the shore; man's spirit rends
Its quiet only up against the ends
Of wants and oppositions, loves and hates,
Where worked and worn by passionate debates,
And losing by the loss it apprehends,
The flesh rocks round, and every breath it sends,
Is ravelled to a sigh. All tortured states
Suppose a straightened place. Jehovah Lord,
Make room for rest, around me! Out of sight
Now float me, of the vexing land abhorred,
Till, in deep calms of space, my soul may right
Her nature; shoot large sail on lengthening cord,
And rush exultant on the Infinite.

## THE BEST THING IN THE WORLD

What's the best thing in the world?
June-rose by May-dew impearled;
Sweet south-wind, that means no rain;
Truth, not cruel to a friend;
Pleasure, not in haste to end;
Beauty, not self-decked and curled
Till its pride is over-plain;
Light, that never makes you wink;
Memory, that gives no pain;
Love, when, *so,* you're loved again.
What's the best thing in the world?
— Something out of it, I think.

Designed by Myron McVay.

Set in photocomposed Garamond, a typeface designed by
Claude Garamond (1480-1561), the first type founder to
establish his own foundry.

Printed on Hallmark Eggshell Book paper.